D1294556

In the Kitchen

Let's Make Bread

By Mary Hill

Welcome Books

Children's Press®
A Division of Scholastic Inc.
New York / Toronto / London / Auckland / Sydney
Mexico City / New Delhi / Hong Kong
Danbury, Connecticut

Photo Credits: Cover and all photos by Maura B. McConnell
Contributing Editor: Jennifer Silate
Book Design: Mindy Liu

Library of Congress Cataloging-in-Publication Data

Hill, Mary, 1977–
    Let's make bread / by Mary Hill
    p. cm. -- (In the kitchen)
    Includes index.
    Summary: Photographs and simple text introduce the steps involved in making a loaf
    of bread.
    ISBN 0-516-23955-4 (lib. bdg.) -- ISBN 0-516-24018-8 (pbk.)
    1. Bread--Juvenile literature. [1. Cookery--Bread. 2 Bread.] I. Title. II. Series.

TX769 .H48 2002
641.8'15--dc21

                                        2001047542

Contents

My name is Janet.

Dad and I are going to make bread.

First, we have to make the **dough**.

I put **flour** in a bowl.

Dad pours some water into the bowl.

I put in some **yeast**.

Yeast will make the dough rise.

I **knead** the dough.

I use my hands to knead it.

Dad puts the dough by the warm oven.

We must wait for the dough to **rise**.

The dough has risen!

We must knead it again.

Next, we put the dough in a pan.

It is time to bake the bread.

Dad puts the pan in the oven.

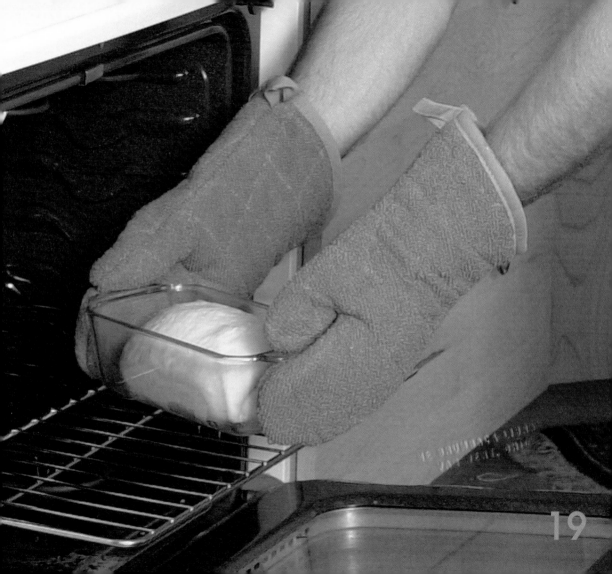

The bread is done.

It tastes good!

New Words

dough (**doh**) a soft, thick mixture of flour, water, and other things, used to make bread, cookies, muffins, and other foods

flour (**flou**-ur) a fine powder made by grinding and sifting a grain

knead (**need**) to press or mix dough into a soft mass

rise (**rize**) to grow larger or lighter

yeast (**yeest**) something that causes dough to rise

To Find Out More

Books
Bread, Bread, Bread
by Ann Morris
William Morrow & Company

Loaves of Fun: A History of Bread with Activities and Recipes from Around the World
by Beth Harbison
Chicago Review Press

Web Site
Botham's Kids Corner
http://www.botham.co.uk/kids.htm
This Web site has recipes, games, and all kinds of information about bread.

Index

About the Author
Mary Hill writes and edits children's books from her home in Maryland.

Reading Consultants

Kris Flynn, Coordinator, Small School District Literacy, The San Diego County Office of Education

Shelly Forys, Certified Reading Recovery Specialist, W.J. Zahnow Elementary School, Waterloo, IL

Sue McAdams, Former President of the North Texas Reading Council of the IRA, and Early Literacy Consultant, Dallas, TX

24